TOUGH GUIDES

HOW TO SURVIVE IN THE DESERT

ANGELA ROYSTON

PowerKiDS press.

New York

Published in 2013 by The Rosen Publishing Group, Inc.
29 East 21st Street, New York, NY 10010

Produced for Rosen by Calcium Creative Ltd
Editors for Calcium Creative Ltd: Sarah Eason and Jennifer Sanderson
US Editor: Sara Antill
Designer: Simon Borrough

Photo credits: Cover: Shutterstock: Photosync, Richard Semik. Inside: Dreamstime: Burt Ayers 28c, R Caucino 22c, Maximus117 7t, Nfsd000 23t; Istockphoto: KLMBK Productions 17tr; Shutterstock: Galyna Andrushko 4l, 4bc, 16l, 28l, Anton Prado Photo 6l, 18l, AP Design 8l, 10l, 20l, 22l, 27c, Joe Belanger 10c, Hagit Berkovich 21t, Amee Cross 25tl, Pichugin Dmitry 5b, 12l, 19bc, 24l, Pierre-Jean Durieu 13l, EuToch 16c, Frontpage 9tr, Hainaultphoto 14c, Hunta 29tl, Rafa Irusta 13r, André Klaassen 26c, Karin Hildebrand Lau 20c, Loskutnikov 15c, Myszka 6c, Seleznev Oleg 18cl, Maxim Petrichuk 12c, Patrick Poendl 8c, Pascal Rateau 14l, 26l, Audrey Snider-Bell 24cl, Guido Vrola 11c.

Library of Congress Cataloging-in-Publication Data

Royston, Angela, 1945–
How to survive in the desert / by Angela Royston.
    p. cm. — (Tough guides)
Includes index.
ISBN 978-1-4488-7867-3 (library binding) — ISBN 978-1-4488-7932-8 (pbk.) — ISBN 978-1-4488-7938-0 (6-pack)
1. Desert survival—Juvenile literature. I. Title.
GV200.5.R67 2013
613.69—dc23

2011052889

CONTENTS

SURVIVING IN THE DESERT

A desert is one of the hardest places to survive. There is little rain, so it is extremely dry and few plants can grow there. Desert plants and animals have special ways of coping with the lack of water, but people must carry water with them.

Sahara

SAHARA
WHERE: covers most of North Africa, an area around the same size as the United States
TEMPERATURE: up to 110° F (43° C) or higher

4

Each desert is different. Some deserts are covered with sand, while others are rocky and stony. The Sahara is the biggest and hottest desert in the world. Not all deserts are hot, though. The Gobi Desert is covered by snow in the winter.

Gobi Desert

TOUGH TIP

Prepare well before traveling into a desert. You could be there for longer than you expect! You may get lost, or, if you are in a vehicle, the vehicle may break down. The worst situation is to end up in a desert by accident, after an airplane crash, for example.

GOBI DESERT
WHERE: Mongolia and northern China
TEMPERATURE: can reach 113° F (45° C) in summer but drops to -40° F (-40° C) in winter

WALK OR STAY?

People who hike into the desert, or drive across it, should know exactly where they are going. Before you start, plan a route and let someone know where you are going and when you expect to arrive. Take a **compass** and maps with you. Even better is a **Global Positioning System device** (GPS) to help you find the way.

the Big Dipper

THE BIG DIPPER

WHAT: a group of stars

FINDING NORTH: draw an imaginary line through the top and left stars (above) to find the **North Star**

6

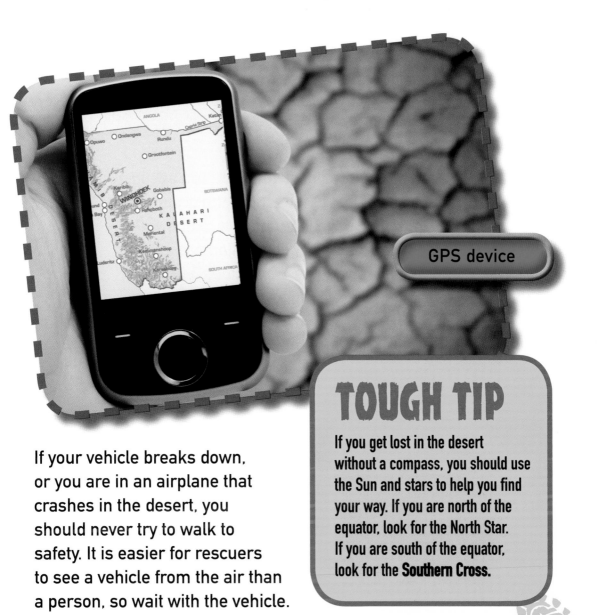

GPS device

If your vehicle breaks down, or you are in an airplane that crashes in the desert, you should never try to walk to safety. It is easier for rescuers to see a vehicle from the air than a person, so wait with the vehicle.

TOUGH TIP

If you get lost in the desert without a compass, you should use the Sun and stars to help you find your way. If you are north of the equator, look for the North Star. If you are south of the equator, look for the **Southern Cross.**

GPS (GLOBAL POSITIONING SYSTEM)
WHAT: gives your exact position
HOW: takes a reading from several satellites in space

7

HIDDEN WATER

There is more water than you can see in a desert. Most of it is under the ground, so people dig wells to reach it. Some water is on the surface, in pools called **oases**. Desert villages, towns, and cities, such as Las Vegas, are built around oases.

oasis

OASIS
WORLD'S BIGGEST: the Nile River is a huge oasis! It flows for more than 1,000 miles (1,609 km) through the Sahara
SIGN OF AN OASIS: a group of trees

8

Death Valley

WARNING! Flash Flood Area

Deserts do not get much rain, but when they do, the rain often comes all at once. Within minutes, streams and rivers are filled with rushing water. This is called a flash flood. Heavy rain from mountains and hills far away also causes flash floods.

TOUGH TIP

If you walk along a dry **river bed**, listen for flash floods. If you hear the roar of water, get out of the way fast. If you wait until the water reaches you, it will be too late.

DEATH VALLEY
WHERE: Mojave Desert, California
FLASH FLOODS: deep canyons on the edge of the Sierra Nevadas give rise to many flash floods in Death Valley

9

HOT AND COLD

Most deserts are baking hot during the day, especially in the summer. Without a cloud in the sky, the Sun beats down all day. These deserts can become cold at night, when the heat from the ground escapes into the air. As the Sun sets, the temperature drops lower and lower.

saguaro cactus

SAGUARO CACTUS
WHERE: Sonoran Desert in southwest United States
SURVIVAL: stores water in its long stems, which grow up to 60 feet (18.2 m) tall

10

You need clothes that are suitable in the heat and the cold. Desert tribespeople wear long, loose clothes that cover their body and stop the Sun from burning their skin. At night, they wrap a blanket around their clothes.

I SURVIVED

Henry Morello was 84 years old when he got lost and drove into a ditch in the Arizona desert. He drank the water from the windshield washer holder. At night he covered himself with the mats in his car. He survived for five days before he was found.

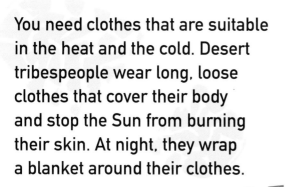

Berber tribesman

BERBER TRIBESPEOPLE
WHERE: Sahara, North Africa
SURVIVAL: stay inside tents during the hottest parts of the day. Wear loose clothing that keeps them cool and covers their heads.

11

WHAT TO TAKE

Desert travelers have to take everything they need with them. You should not take anything that you cannot carry. Wear loose clothes, a sun hat or scarf, sunglasses, and strong boots. Use high-factor sunscreen to protect any bare skin.

drinking water

DRINKING WATER
HOW MUCH: drink at least 1 gallon (3.8 l) per day
WHY: you lose much more water than usual in the hot, dry desert. The body is 80 percent water and can easily dry out.

12

Equipment can be heavy and bulky, but some things are necessary. They include a tent and sleeping bag, matches for lighting a fire, and pots for cooking. Most important are maps, a compass, and GPS for finding the way. A mirror is useful, too, for lighting fires.

TOUGH TIP

Water is precious in the desert. Do not waste it on things such as washing up. Do what desert tribespeople do, and clean dirty dishes by rubbing them with sand.

desert gear

DESERT GEAR
TENT: provides shelter from the Sun during the day and from the cold at night
STRONG BOOTS: for walking long distances

13

WATER AND FOOD

Anyone traveling into the desert must take enough water and food to last them for the whole time, or until they reach the next oasis. Hikers can last only a short time. People who have camels to carry their bags or who are driving can take enough water to last for several days.

camels

CAMEL
HUMP: a store of fat that the camel's body breaks down to make water
FACT: can last for a month without water

14

Water is more important than food. You can survive three weeks without food, but in the desert you can hardly survive a day without water. Dried fruit and energy bars are good to take.

TOUGH TIP

If you see what looks like a pool of water where you do not expect it, do not try to reach it. It is almost certainly a **mirage**, not an oasis. Remember that an oasis has plants growing around it.

mirage

MIRAGE
WHAT: the reflection of a patch of sky, caused by a trick of the light
HOW: it moves away as you walk toward it

15

DYING OF THIRST

Running out of water is very serious in the desert. Thirst is the first sign that your body is **dehydrated**, which means that it is short of water. If you are thirsty and do not drink, you will soon get a headache, and feel sick and dizzy. It is more important to keep drinking small amounts of water than to save it for later.

prickly pear cactus

PRICKLY PEAR CACTUS
FRUIT: can be eaten, but remove the prickles first
USE: stem contains water and can be eaten raw or cooked

I SURVIVED

Matthew McGough and his young daughter Shannon were stranded in the Australian desert for seven days after their car broke down. They drank the water from the car's **radiator**, but then they had nothing. When they were rescued, Matthew drank 3 gallons (11.3 l) of water in five minutes. Shannon drank 1 gallon (3.8 l) of water.

Aborigine

As the thirst becomes worse, your mouth becomes dry. When people become dangerously dehydrated, they begin to lose their reasoning. They see things that are not there and may wander off into the desert, leaving everything behind.

ABORIGINE TRIBESPEOPLE
WHERE: the Australian desert
SURVIVAL: collect dew from plants in early morning before it is evaporated by the Sun

17

SHELTER FROM THE HEAT

Becoming too hot is as dangerous as running out of water. Midday is the hottest time of day. Travelers should try to keep as cool as possible. Look for shade under large rocks or put up a tent.

desert tent

DESERT TENT
WHAT: used by Berber tribespeople for shelter and to stay cool
MATERIAL: made of camel and goat hair to keep out heat

18

Desert animals avoid the hot Sun. Snakes and spiders may find shelter under stones, but many animals have underground burrows. Gerbils and hamsters, for example, stay cool in their tunnels during the day and come out at night to find food.

TOUGH TIP

If you are hiking or traveling in the desert, get up early and start moving as soon as it is light. Then rest in the middle of the day and move again in the evening, when the temperature has cooled down.

desert lizard

LIZARD
WHAT: a reptile
SURVIVAL: warms up in the sunshine and darts into the shade before it gets too hot

HEATSTROKE

Most of the time your body keeps itself cool. The hotter you get, the more you sweat. However, if your temperature rises above 105° F (42° C), your body can no longer keep itself cool. This is called **heatstroke**, and it can be fatal.

water tube

WATER PACK
WHAT: worn on the back or around the neck
HOW: has a tube for sipping water

20

fennec fox

TOUGH TIP

To avoid heatstroke, keep covered! Your clothes will soak up your sweat and, as they dry, will help to cool you down. Be sure to wear light-colored clothes. Dark colors absorb heat, but light colors reflect it and keep you cooler.

Early signs of heatstroke include feeling dizzy and being sick. As people overheat, their heart beats very quickly, they breathe very fast, and become confused. They may see and hear things that are not there, and they can pass out. Someone with heatstroke needs to be cooled down immediately.

FENNEC FOX
WHERE: Sahara and Arabian Deserts
SURVIVAL: large ears that allow heat to escape, thick fur that protects the skin from the Sun

21

KEEPING WARM

As soon as the Sun goes down, the temperature begins to drop. Now is the time to light a fire and set up camp. A fire helps to keep you warm and allows you to cook food or boil water for a hot drink.

camp fire

CAMP FIRE
WHY: temperature can drop from 100° F (37.8° C) to 50° F (10° C) or lower
BURN: dry twigs and camel dung

gerbil

TOUGH TIP

You need a blanket to keep you warm at night. The best kind of blanket is a special silver one that protects you from the cold. It weighs very little and folds up small. Do not forget to hang a mosquito net across the tent door to keep out the insects.

Try to make your bed a few feet above the ground so that snakes cannot bite you as you sleep. If possible, hang a hammock inside your tent. Desert animals need to keep warm at night, too. Mammals, such as foxes, gerbils, and camels, have thick fur to keep them warm.

GERBIL
WHERE: deserts in Africa and Asia
SURVIVAL: lives underground in burrows and feeds at night

23

POISONOUS BITES AND STINGS

A desert looks empty, but do not be fooled. It is buzzing with flies and other insects. The most dangerous insect is a mosquito, because it carries a deadly disease called **malaria**. Rub **insect repellent** onto your skin during the day and at night.

scorpion

SCORPION
WHERE: every continent except Antarctica
THREAT: poisonous sting at the end of the tail kills or paralyzes **prey**

24

rattlesnake

TOUGH TIP

Before you put on your boots in the morning, check that a poisonous spider has not climbed into one of them overnight. Turn each boot upside down and shake it. If anyone is bitten by a poisonous spider or snake, get help fast. Remember exactly what the creature looks like so the correct **antidote** can be given.

Insects are not the only threat in the desert. **Scorpions**, snakes, and spiders live there, too. They are often hard to spot because their skin is well **camouflaged** against the ground. One of the most dangerous snakes is a rattlesnake. Its tail rattles as it moves, so listen for it and keep out of its way!

RATTLESNAKE
WHERE: North, Central, and South America
THREAT: two fangs squeeze poison into any flesh it bites

25

SANDSTORMS

It is often windy in the desert. Strong winds can whip up the sand or dust into a thick cloud, which moves across the desert. When it hits you, the sand stings your skin and gets into everything, including your eyes, mouth, boots, and rucksack.

sandstorm

SANDSTORM
WHERE: the Sahara and Arabian Deserts
SIZE: severe **sandstorms** can create a wall of sand up to 5,000 feet (1,524 m) high

Sandstorms are dangerous. The cloud of sand is so thick, you cannot see where you are going, and you cannot hear above the noise of the wind. It is easy to lose your way, or to become separated from your companions. The safest thing to do is to find shelter until the storm ends.

I SURVIVED

Mauro Prosperi was taking part in a six-day run through the Sahara, when he ran into a sandstorm. He could not see and ran off the route by mistake. He survived for nine days by eating bats and snakes. He was found 186 miles (299 km) away from where he should have been.

keffiyeh

KEFFIYEH
WHAT: long piece of material that can be wound around the head to cover the hair, nose, mouth, and ears
WHY: protects head and face from sunburn and sandstorms

27

RESCUE

How do you get help in an emergency? If you are stranded, make a signal that is easy to see, particularly from the air. Spread out a large, colored sheet on the ground. If an airplane flies overhead, use a mirror to catch the sunlight to send a signal.

rescue helicopter

RESCUE HELICOPTER
WHY: rescuers in the air can cover a lot of ground searching for missing people
USE: can easily land and pick up people

28

local guide

Most people are rescued by other travelers or local people who happen to find them. Lighting a fire will make smoke that can be seen from the ground and the air. The best way to stay safe in the desert is to travel in a group with a local guide.

I SURVIVED

In 2007, Charles Wooler was forced to land his airplane in the Kalahari Desert when he lost his way. After waiting by the airplane for two days, he left a note explaining that he was walking south. A rescue party found his note and used tracker dogs to follow his footsteps until they found him two days later.

LOCAL GUIDE
WHAT: person who knows where there is water and safe routes
USE: people use camels to carry supplies and people who are sick or injured

29

GLOSSARY

antidote (AN-tih-doht) A medicine that undoes the harmful effects of a poison.

camouflaged (KA-muh-flahjd) Colored or patterned to match the surroundings.

compass (KUM-pus) A device that shows the direction of north.

dehydrated (dee-HY-drayt-ed) Containing less water than normal.

dung (DUNG) Animal waste.

fangs (FANGZ) Long, sharp teeth.

Global Positioning System device (GLOH-bul puh-ZIH-shun-ing SIS-tum dih-VYS) A device that helps find your location on a map.

heatstroke (HEET-strohk) When the temperature of the body is so high the body can no longer cool itself.

insect repellent (In-sekt rih-PEH-lunt) A cream or spray that stops insects from biting you.

malaria (muh-LER-ee-uh) A dangerous disease that is passed to animals and people when an infected mosquito bites them.

mirage (muh-RAJ) A trick of light that makes it look as if there is water on the ground when there is not.

North Star (NORTH STAHR) A star that is always directly above the North Pole and so gives the direction of north.

oases (oh-AY-seez) Places in the desert where there is water.

prey (PRAY) An animal that is hunted and eaten by other animals.

radiator (RAY-dee-ay-ter) A container through which water flows.

river bed (RIH-ver BED) A channel that a river flows along.

sandstorms (SAND-storm) Strong winds that blow large amounts of sand.

scorpions (SKOR-pee-un) Animals that are closely related to spiders.

Southern Cross (SUH-thern KROS) A group of stars in the southern hemisphere from which you can find the direction of south.

30

FURTHER READING

Dell, Pamela. *Surviving Death Valley: Desert Adaptation.* Mankato, MN: Capstone Press, 2008.

Lynette, Rachel. *Who Lives in a Hot, Dry Desert?.* Exploring Habitats. New York: PowerKids Press, 2011.

Pipe, Jim. *Desert Survival.* Extreme Habitats. New York: Gareth Stevens, 2008.

Sandler, Michael. *Deserts: Surviving in the Sahara.* X-Treme Places. New York: Bearport Publishing, 2006.

WEBSITES

Due to the changing nature of Internet links, PowerKids Press has developed an online list of websites related to the subject of this book. This site is updated regularly. Please use this link to access the list:
www.powerkidslinks.com/guide/desert/

INDEX